EPHESIANS

LIVING IN GOD'S HOUSEHOLD

11 Studies for Individuals or Groups

R O B E R T   B A Y L I S

SHAW

EPHESIANS
A SHAW BOOK
PUBLISHED BY WATERBROOK PRESS
5446 North Academy Boulevard, Suite 200
Colorado Springs, CO 80918
A division of Random House, Inc.

Unless otherwise indicated, all Scripture quotations are taken from the *Holy Bible: New International Version* ® *NIV* ® Copyright © 1973, 1978, 1984 by International Bible Society. Used by permission of Zondervan Publishing House. All rights reserved.

ISBN: 0-87788-223-1

SHAW and its circle of books logo are trademarks
of WaterBrook Press, a division of Random House, Inc.

Printed in the United States of America

03 02 01 00

15 14 13 12

CONTENTS

INTRODUCTION

Sometime in the years A.D. 62–63 a man fettered with a chain sat in a house in the imperial city of Rome. He was composing a letter. He was under close guard because he was charged with sedition, a very serious political crime. This man, the great apostle Paul, was a prolific and gifted writer. Eventually he would be recognized as the foremost expositor of Christian truth in all history.

Paul had spent much of his Christian life on the move and constantly under attack because of his courageous and uncompromising preaching of the Christian gospel. Often his correspondence had to deal with the false teachings and improper behavior that had seeped into the churches. Thus, most of Paul's letters that have come down to us in the New Testament are arguments in defense of the truth, addressed to a specific church and written in a style that reflects the pressures of limited time and heavy responsibility.

Now, at the time of his prison writing, most of his public life lay in the past, and Paul had time on his hands to reflect. He had, not long before, written an epistle to the church at Colossae dealing with a particular heresy. In that letter he had developed the thought that all the fullness of God resided in Christ, and that Christ was sufficient to meet every spiritual need. Apparently that idea was still with him as he began this new letter.

What the apostle Paul wrote (later misnamed the Epistle to the Ephesians) was in one sense his greatest work of literature. It was probably a general letter, a kind of grand summation of all that he had ever taught, intended to make the rounds of all the churches in Asia Minor. In it he expresses, with almost poetic quality, the great theme of the unity of all things in Jesus Christ and describes how one-time strangers are now invited to live together as one, in God's household.

A good reason for reading the letter to the Ephesians is that, as we pointed out earlier, it distills the deepest of Paul's teachings about Jesus Christ and his church. This book is a very direct way of finding out who Jesus Christ is, what his purposes are for mankind (including us), and how these purposes can be carried out in our lives day by day amid the ordinary circumstances of human existence.

HOW TO USE THIS STUDYGUIDE

Fisherman studyguides are based on the inductive approach to Bible study. Inductive study is discovery study; we discover what the Bible says as we ask questions about its content and search for answers. This is quite different from the process in which a teacher *tells* a group *about* the Bible and what it means and what to do about it. In inductive study God speaks directly to each of us through his Word.

A group functions best when a leader keeps the discussion on target, but this leader is neither the teacher nor the "answer person." A leader's responsibility is to *ask*—not *tell*. The answers come from the text itself as group members examine, discuss, and think together about the passage.

There are four kinds of questions in each study. The first is an *approach question*. Used before the Bible passage is read, this question breaks the ice and helps you focus on the topic of the Bible study. It begins to reveal where thoughts and feelings need to be transformed by Scripture.

Some of the earlier questions in each study are *observation questions* designed to help you find out basic facts—who, what, where, when, and how.

When you know what the Bible says you need to ask, *What does it mean?* These *interpretation questions* help you to discover the writer's basic message.

Application questions ask, *What does it mean to me?* They challenge you to live out the Scripture's life-transforming message.

Fisherman studyguides provide spaces between questions for jotting down responses and related questions you would like to raise in the group. Each group member should have a copy of the studyguide and may take a turn in leading the group.

A group should use any accurate, modern translation of the Bible such as the *New International Version,* the *New American Standard Bible,* the *Revised Standard Version,* the *New Jerusalem Bible,* or the *Good News Bible.* (Other translations or paraphrases of the Bible may be referred to when additional help is needed.) Bible commentaries should not be brought to a Bible study because they tend to dampen discussion and keep people from thinking for themselves.

SUGGESTIONS FOR GROUP LEADERS

1. Read and study the Bible passage thoroughly beforehand, grasping its themes and applying its teachings for yourself. Pray that the Holy Spirit will "guide you into truth" so that your leadership will guide others.

2. If the studyguide's questions ever seem ambiguous or unnatural to you, rephrase them, feeling free to add others that seem necessary to bring out the meaning of a verse.

3. Begin (and end) the study promptly. Start by asking someone to pray for God's help. Remember, the Holy Spirit is the teacher, not you!

4. Ask for volunteers to read the passages out loud.

5. As you ask the studyguide's questions in sequence, encourage everyone to participate in the discussion. If some are silent, ask, "What do you think, Heather?" or, "Dan, what can you add to that answer?" or suggest, "Let's have an answer from someone who hasn't spoken up yet."

6. If a question comes up that you can't answer, don't be afraid to admit that you're baffled! Assign the topic as a research project for someone to report on next week.

7. Keep the discussion moving and focused. Though tangents will inevitably be introduced, you can bring the discussion back to the topic at hand. Learn to pace the discussion so that you finish a study each session you meet.

8. Don't be afraid of silences: some questions take time to answer and some people need time to gather courage to speak. If silence persists, rephrase your question, but resist the temptation to answer it yourself.

9. If someone comes up with an answer that is clearly illogical or unbiblical, ask him or her for further clarification: "What verse suggests that to you?"

10. Discourage Bible-hopping and overuse of cross-references. Learn all you can from *this* passage, along with a few important references suggested in the studyguide.

11. Some questions are marked with a ♦. This indicates that further information is available in the Leader's Notes at the back of the guide.

12. For further information on getting a new Bible study group started and keeping it functioning effectively, read Gladys Hunt's *You Can Start a Bible Study Group* and *Pilgrims in Progress: Growing through Groups* by Jim and Carol Plueddemann.

SUGGESTIONS FOR GROUP MEMBERS

1. Learn and apply the following ground rules for effective Bible study. (If new members join the group later, review these guidelines with the whole group.)

2. Remember that your goal is to learn all that you can *from the Bible passage being studied.* Let it speak for itself without using Bible commentaries or other Bible passages. There is more than enough in each assigned passage to keep your group productively occupied for one session. Sticking to the passage saves the group from insecurity and confusion.

3. Avoid the temptation to bring up those fascinating tangents that don't really grow out of the passage you are discussing. If the topic is of common interest, you can bring it up later in informal conversation following the study. Meanwhile, help each other stick to the subject!

4. Encourage each other to participate. People remember best what they discover and verbalize for themselves. Some people are naturally shyer than others, or they may be afraid of making a mistake. If your discussion is free and friendly and you show real interest in what other group members think and feel, they will be more likely to speak up. Remember, the more people involved in a discussion, the richer it will be.

5. Guard yourself from answering too many questions or talking too much. Give others a chance to express themselves. If you are one who participates easily, discipline yourself by counting to ten before you open your mouth!

6. Make personal, honest applications and commit yourself to letting God's Word change you.

A PLAN FOR THE FULLNESS OF TIME

Ephesians 1:1-14

The story goes that two men had a contest to see which one of them could plow the straightest furrow in the field. When the contest was over, two furrows went the length of the field. One wobbled from right to left; the other was perfectly straight. When the winner was asked his secret, he said, "I just kept my eyes on that fence post at the end of the field."

Sometimes knowing where we will finish can help us keep a straighter course in the meantime. The opening verses of Ephesians give us some startling pictures of who we are as Christians and what destiny God has designed for us.

1. Describe one or two major goals you have for your life.

Read Ephesians 1:1-14.

♦ **2.** The opening words in the hymn (verses 3-4) pronounce a blessing on God for having blessed us and chosen us *in Christ.* What do you think "in Christ" means in this context?

What do you think Paul means by "the heavenly realms"? (Watch for this phrase, which reappears throughout the letter.)

3. What appears to be the purpose for which God has blessed and chosen us?

4. The second stanza (verses 5-6) deals with God's predetermined plan for us. What is each Christian's destiny?

♦ *Indicates further information in Leader's Notes*

5. What is the means by which this destiny is brought about?

◆ **6.** Stanza three (verses 7-8) concerns two vital gifts that are received through Christ: *redemption* and *forgiveness*. What do you know about these two aspects of the Christian faith?

How are these two gifts related?

7. The hymn reaches its high point in stanza four, made up of verses 9-10. God has revealed the mystery of his will "when the times will have reached their fulfillment." What does this phrase imply?

What is the plan?

8. The next stanza (verses 11-12) brings us into the picture. How do we "who were the first to hope in Christ" fit into God's plan?

9. Finally, stanza six (verses 13-14) takes us back to God again (the hymn begins and ends with God) by showing that he has guaranteed our inheritance. How does he do this? Does this mean anything to you personally?

10. Look back through these six stanzas. What nouns and verbs does Paul use to show that nothing God has done for us is mere coincidence or happenstance? What time span is covered in verses 3-14?

11. How does the individual Christian's destiny fit into God's plan?

12. As you begin to understand your part in the "bigger picture," how can this knowledge make a difference in your day-to-day life?

STUDY 2

THE APOSTLE'S PRAYER

Ephesians 1:15-23

The act of prayer is accepted as a matter of course in most Christian circles, and most Christians make an effort to pray for one another. Yet their prayers often revolve around physical or material needs: health, finances, decisions about where to live or what job to take. Paul's prayer for his spiritual family gives us reason to reevaluate the emphases of our prayers.

1. What kind of prayer requests do you make regularly for yourself and those close to you?

Read Ephesians 1:15-23.

◆ **2.** Why was Paul continually thankful for these Christians?

3. In verse 17 Paul begins a special prayer request. Why is this such a crucial request?

Do you feel you need to make this request now? Write in your own words what Paul is asking.

4. Paul specifies three requests that he desires these Christians to know once the "eyes of [their hearts]" have been opened (verses 18-19). Can you explain these three things in terms of what they mean to you, right now?

5. What is the supreme demonstration of the "incomparably great power" of God (verses 19-20)?

♦ **6.** After God raised Jesus from the dead, where did he place him? What does this reveal to us about who Jesus is?

7. According to verse 22, how is the church related to Jesus?

8. In a world where so many religions exist, what is the significance of the statements in verses 20-23?

9. What does Jesus' position in the universe mean to you personally?

10. What aspects of Jesus' position are you most likely to forget sometimes, and how does that affect your daily life?

LIFE OUT OF DEATH

Ephesians 2:1-10

One woman was discussing the importance of religious training for children. She related with some dismay an incident in which her young son was playing with children who represented other religious groups. One child claimed to be Episcopalian, another Jewish. Her son proudly announced that he was "Chicagoan."

In a world where diversity exists, not merely between nations, but right in the neighborhood, the Christian must ask himself what faith in Christ really means. Paul was writing to Christians who were a minority and living in a culture where many groups collided. He was careful to point out the real difference between those "in Christ" and those who had not yet been reborn in their spirits.

1. What do you see as a major difference between Christians and non-Christians?

Read Ephesians 2:1-3.

2. The first two sentences in this chapter sum up what it means to be a non-Christian. Using terms that a non-religious person could understand, explain what it means to be spiritually "dead."

3. What and who were we following when we were spiritually dead (verse 2)?

Describe some "ways of this world" and how they influence you.

♦ **4.** How have you perceived your life to be affected by "the ruler of the kingdom of the air"?

5. List some "cravings of our sinful nature" (verse 3). (Remember that *nature* refers to the whole person, not just our physical selves.)

◆ **6.** Why do you think Paul uses the terms "disobedient" and "objects of wrath" to describe how we were (verses 2-3)? How are these terms related?

Read Ephesians 2:4-10.

7. The solution to the way we all once lived is found in verses 4-7, beginning with the key transition phrase "But . . . God." List the three main things that God has done for us.

8. The phrase "with Christ" or "with him" also appears three times in these verses. How does this phrase add to the meaning of what God has done?

9. What is God's purpose, beyond our own personal benefit, in making us alive with Christ (verse 7)?

◆ **10.** Define *grace* and *faith*. (Get help from the dictionary if necessary.)

11. Explain the relationship between grace and faith expressed in verse 8. Whose is the grace? Whose is the faith?

What part does each of these qualities play in salvation?

12. Notice the play on words in verses 9-10: *works, workmanship,* then *works* again. What does the word *works* mean as used here?

How does the word *workmanship* create a distinction between the first *works* and the later *works*?

13. Which kind of works do you find yourself doing the most? Why? Pray together for a fuller understanding of God's grace and what it means to be alive in Christ.

THE END OF OLD HOSTILITIES

Ephesians 2:11-22

History, on both the small and large scale, plays an important part in our understanding of the Christian faith. Because some Christian Jews maintained that they had a superior relationship with God, it was important for Paul to explain to the Jews how they had failed to serve God as a nation in the past. It was also important for him to explain to the Gentiles that they could now enjoy a personal relationship with God even though they were not part of the "chosen people."

1. What does it mean to be alienated? And how does alienation affect us?

Read Ephesians 2:11-13.

♦ **2.** In what ways were the Ephesians once alienated from God?

3. Does the description in verse 12 match your own experience in any way? Explain.

4. In verse 13 Paul sets forth the dramatic contrast between past and present with the words "But now . . ." What brings us near to God?

Read Ephesians 2:14-18.

◆ **5.** How did Christ make peace between Jew and Gentile?

◆ **6.** How could abolishing the law remove the barrier between Jew and Gentile (verse 15)?

How did Christ reconcile both groups to God?

7. A further bond of peace between Gentiles and Jews is mentioned in verses 17-18. Discuss verse 18 in terms of what it means and how it can be true for us now.

Read Ephesians 2:19-22.

8. Paul says that we are citizens as well as members of God's household. What are the advantages of citizenship? Of belonging to a family?

9. Does this illustration help you to understand your place in the household of faith now? Why?

♦ **10.** What is our household built on, and who is the cornerstone?

Why is this foundation so important?

11. According to verses 21-22, what is the goal of bringing us all together?

12. How can an emphasis on unity help in your relationship with . . .

God?

church?

friends?

enemies?

family?

employer/employees?

A MYSTERY REVEALED

Ephesians 3

Even a brief glance at a television listing on any given day will indicate how much people are intrigued by the unknown. There are programs about crimes that haven't been solved, missing people who haven't been found, strange "sightings" yet to be explained, and weird stories yet to be disproved. People have a natural hunger for mystery.

Paul attempts in this part of his letter to help his readers understand the mystery of what God has accomplished through the life, death, and resurrection of Jesus Christ. Although these spiritual realities will never be fully comprehended by humans this side of heaven, they provide us with much to ponder—and should stir us to long even more after knowledge of God and his plan.

1. In explaining Christianity to a nonbeliever, what would you say is the "main point" of the faith?

Read Ephesians 3:1-13.

2. What is the mystery Paul speaks of in verses 2-6?

How did Paul learn of this mystery?

3. Why is this truth referred to as a mystery?

4. For what task did Paul receive grace (verses 7-9)?

5. Why would Paul need particular grace for this (remember the issues raised in chapter 2)?

6. What further light does Paul throw on the mystery in verse 10?

7. What do you think *church* means, as used in verse 10? What is the church's purpose as described here?

Would the popular understanding of what a church is fit this context?

8. What refreshing news do we hear in verse 12? What does this mean to you personally?

♦ **9.** Why might these believers have been disheartened, and on what basis does Paul encourage them?

Read Ephesians 3:14-21.

10. What do we learn about our own spiritual needs in these prayer requests of Paul?

11. What do we learn about God's resources for us?

12. What do we learn about God's love?

13. Is there an aspect of this prayer you would especially emphasize for yourself or for family and friends? Close with silent prayer.

THE GIFTS OF CHRIST

Ephesians 4:1-16

The first gift a Christian receives is the gift of the Holy Spirit. He comes to everyone who opens his or her life to Jesus Christ. He works in our lives, deepening our love for Jesus, honing our abilities, and giving us spiritual gifts for service in the church. Paul encourages us in this passage to work toward unity and growth, each of us doing our part in the body of Christ.

1. What do you see as your spiritual gifts, and how are you using them?

Read Ephesians 4:1-7.

2. Paul begins this part of his letter by urging his readers to bring their lives up to the standards of their calling. What *is* our calling?

♦ **3.** Critics of Christianity often point out the external divisions between various groups of Christians. On the basis of verses 1-6, how would you answer such a criticism?

4. According to verse 7, who has received grace? Who determines how much grace we receive?

What do you conclude is the message to each of us in this statement?

Read Ephesians 4:8-16.

5. In the next three verses Paul quotes from Psalm 68:18 and follows it with an explanation of the term *ascended* used in the passage quoted. What knowledge about "ascending" and "descending" would have been lacking for a reader of the psalm who knew only the Old Testament?

6. What is Paul trying to clarify about the gifts of Christ through this quote and explanation?

7. Paul now specifies the gifts that Christ has bestowed on the church. Why are these jobs or responsibilities to be looked upon as gifts?

♦ **8.** Define *apostle, prophet, evangelist, pastor,* and *teacher* in terms of what these individuals do.

9. The teaching about gifts ends in verses 13-16 with an explanation of their purpose. What is that purpose?

10. What is the definition of maturity, according to verse 13?

11. What do we avoid by becoming mature (verse 14)?

12. What is the ultimate result of maturity?

13. In what practical way can you apply the principles of this study passage to the development and use of your own gifts?

THE OLD AND NEW NATURES

Ephesians 4:17-32

Spiritual truth is difficult to apply unless given a familiar shape; thus the Christian life has been explained through the use of all sorts of metaphors, illustrations, and parables. Here Paul uses the simple act of getting dressed to help believers grasp their own responsibility in growth and change.

1. Have you ever tried to begin a good habit or break a bad one? How did you do it?

Read Ephesians 4:17-19.

2. According to Paul, the Gentiles live "in the futility of their thinking." What does this phrase tell us about the life of those unfamiliar with God?

3. Specific charges are brought against the Gentiles in verses 18-19. Restate them in your own words. Are the charges still true about people who are not Christians?

Read Ephesians 4:20-24.

4. One of the most difficult questions for anyone to answer adequately is *What is truth?* Paul gives one answer in verses 20-21. What is the answer?

How does this answer differ from our usual concept of truth?

5. Paul applies his statement about truth to the question of behavior by using the metaphor of garments that are "put off" and "put on." Discuss the process of putting on the new nature.

6. In this process of putting on the new nature, what is made new (verse 23)? How do you think this happens?

7. What description of the "new self" do you find in verse 24?

Read Ephesians 4:25-32.

8. The remainder of the chapter consists of concrete advice on how a person can allow the new nature to be *worked out* in daily living. Discuss each piece of advice in terms of how you can apply it now. (Notice that these statements are imperative—they are commands. Paul doesn't leave any room for quibbling!)

♦ **9.** The command in verse 30 concerning the Holy Spirit is a little less easy to grasp than the others. The two key words are *grieve* and *sealed*. Try to help one another understand this statement by defining these two words.

10. How might the instructions of verses 31-32 be key in the command of verse 30?

11. How might we help one another change "garments"— out of our old way of life and into the new nature of Christ?

WALKING IN THE LIGHT

Ephesians 5:1-21

Light and darkness are very important symbols in the New Testament. Jesus is called the "true light that gives light to every man" (John 1:9). The effect of the moral light brought into the world by Jesus can clearly be seen in history. The darkness of human evil is most intense where the light sent from God either has not penetrated or is deliberately shut out. This part of the letter to the Ephesians deals very specifically with some of the central issues of "walking in the light."

1. Relate an experience you've had of being in the presence of someone who seemed evil to you, or relate an experience of being with someone you considered holy.

Read Ephesians 5:1-14.

2. The last part of chapter 4 and the first part of chapter 5 contain details of what it means to put on the new nature. A summary of this teaching comes in chapter 5:1-2, and consists of two commands. In your own words, state the essence of these two commands.

3. Two kinds of people are contrasted in verses 3-14. Who are they? What are the characteristics of each? What is the ultimate destiny of each?

4. What does Paul say about the relationship the "children of light" (verse 8) should have to "those who are disobedient" (verse 6)?

♦ **5.** Notice how often the words *light* and *darkness* appear in these verses. What can be expected of those who live in darkness? Of those who live in God's light?

6. What is the Christian's motivation for doing right (verse 10)?

Read Ephesians 5:15-21.

7. Paul develops at least three contrasts, showing how the walk of a believer in Christ should differ from that of an unbeliever. List them below.

8. What practical means do believers have of encouraging one another (verses 19-20)?

9. How does submitting to one another affect our life together and the maturing process?

10. Relate some examples in your experience of submitting to other believers. What is difficult about submitting? What is rewarding about it?

11. In what way can you allow your own "light" to shine brighter?

THE MARRIAGE RELATIONSHIP

Ephesians 5:22-33

One of the truths most effectively suppressed by the evil one is the biblical view of marriage and the relationship between the sexes. In the first century this truth had been largely lost by the Jews, who considered wives as articles of property with few legal rights. In Greek and Roman societies, the kind of fidelity in marriage taught by the Bible was unknown. Today the world generally believes that the Bible teaches "puritanical repression" of sexual relationship and that male chauvinism is a Christian doctrine. In this passage Paul offers the true biblical outlook on marriage, and even Christians may find it contains some surprises as they learn more about living in God's household.

1. How has Christian faith affected your marriage, or the marriage of someone you know?

Read Ephesians 5:22-33.

♦ **2.** How does the illustration of Christ and the church make clear the relationship of the wife to her husband?

With this illustration in mind, tell in practical terms what *submit* means, and what it does not mean.

3. The truth about Christ and the church is applied to husbands in verses 25-27. List below the ways in which Christ loved the church.

Now apply these ways to how a husband should love his wife.

4. The parallel between the spiritual and the practical is made in verse 28. Summarize this idea below.

5. Verses 29-32 drive home a fundamental truth, one found throughout the Bible (note the quotation from Genesis 2:24). What is this truth, which Paul calls a "profound mystery"?

6. How are the physical and the spiritual harmonized in this teaching?

Is there any danger of one or another of these aspects of the marriage union getting out of balance? Explain.

7. Notice that Paul ends with a mutual admonition. What does this imply about the responsibility for keeping a Christian marriage in balance?

8. Although "dating" did not exist in Paul's day, how could the lessons of this study apply to a dating relationship? How would a dating relationship differ from the married relationship, where these principles are concerned?

9. What principles from this lesson are most challenging to you, and why? How might you apply them to your own relationships?

CHILDREN AND PARENTS, SLAVES AND MASTERS

Ephesians 6:1-9

In Paul's day, no Roman citizen did menial tasks. All such work was done by slaves, who had no more rights than tools or machinery. Children, too, were under the absolute power of their fathers. Though the rights of workers, women, and children are the subject of much political activity in the Western world today, there is still far more abuse than most people realize. Against this contemporary social backdrop, Paul's admonition and advice have a unique timelessness, and present standards for domestic relationships to which every generation can relate.

1. Has being a Christian affected your behavior as an employer or employee? Explain.

Read Ephesians 6:1-4.

2. In considering the marriage relationship previously, the key verb was *submit*. What key verb is directed toward children and slaves?

Is there a difference between these verbs? What is it?

3. In verses 2-3 Paul quotes from the Old Testament law, Exodus 20:12 and Deuteronomy 5:16. Define the word *honor* as used here, putting it in practical terms that spell out some action.

4. What is the significance to us now of the promise cited in verse 3?

♦ **5.** The advice to fathers is both negative and positive. How can these two admonitions be kept in balance?

Read Ephesians 6:5-9.

♦ **6.** Paul directed his remarks in verses 5-8 to a very large segment of the population of his own society. To whom could they be applied today? How?

7. What attitude and actions are slaves to have (verses 5-7)?

8. Toward whom should this attitude focus, and why (verses 7-8)?

9. Again, the admonition ends in verse 9 with advice both positive and negative (notice that the form is reversed from verse 4). How can this statement be an encouragement to a slave, or the modern equivalent of a slave?

10. What kind of potential for social change do you find in this Scripture passage? How might you apply this teaching to your own involvement in society?

THE CHRISTIAN'S ARMOR

Ephesians 6:10-24

Paul was well acquainted with trouble. When he wrote this letter he was a prisoner in Rome, chained to a soldier day and night. Even with this distraction and hardship, he was able to give some final words of encouragement using an analogy suggested, perhaps, by the uniform and equipment of his guard. Thus was born the concept of the Christian's armor that has been such an inspiration to believers down through the ages.

1. What kinds of trouble have you faced in your spiritual life?

Read Ephesians 6:10-17.

♦ **2.** According to Paul's warning, who or what is the enemy against whom Christians are encouraged to stand?

How realistic is this warning for us in the modern world?

3. Why do you think Paul puts so much emphasis on the word *stand* (verses 13-14)? Why, for example, doesn't he use an active verb like *fight,* or *advance?*

4. Identify each part of the Christian's armor with its allegorical meaning. Which parts are defensive? Offensive?

5. How can you relate and apply these truths to the kind of temptations or problems you are facing this week?

Read Ephesians 6:18-20.

6. What is another important "weapon" we are urged to use? Describe the extent to which God wants us to be individually involved in this warfare in the Spirit.

7. Why do you think a concrete analogy or picture is not given in this case?

8. What do you learn about Paul personally from these remarks?

9. So often a battle is over before we even think of our armor. How can we prepare ourselves beforehand for encounter with the enemy at any time?

Read Ephesians 6:21-24.

10. Why was Paul sending news by way of a personal friend and fellow Christian, rather than merely by a letter-carrier (verses 21-22)? Why is personal contact so important?

11. How does the benediction in verses 23-24 compare with closing notes you include in letters? What is Paul asking for these Christians?

Write your own benediction, or blessing, and try using it in some of your correspondence to other believers.

LEADER'S NOTES

Question 2. Ephesians 1:3-14 comprises a doxology or hymn of praise to God—the Father, Son, and Holy Spirit. In the original Greek it is all one sentence. The language and ideas seem rather complicated in some of our English prose versions, but when the hymn is seen as a unit consisting of six fairly evenly divided stanzas, it is a little easier to handle. Notice further that each stanza has two parallel ideas, and you will find that the hymn is constructed with more care than it first appears. Read the whole unit through and then concentrate on the questions.

Question 6. "Forgiveness is rooted in the nature of God as gracious. But his forgiveness is not indiscriminate. He will 'by no means clear the guilty.' On man's side there is the need for penitence if he is to be forgiven. While this is not put into a formal demand, it is everywhere implied. Penitent sinners are forgiven. Impenitent men, who still go on in their wicked way, are not" *(New Bible Dictionary, Second Edition,* p. 390. Wheaton, Ill.: Tyndale House Publishers, 1982).

"Redemption means deliverance from some evil by payment of a price. It is more than simple deliverance. Thus prisoners of war might be released on payment of a price which was called a 'ransom'. . . . In this circle of ideas Christ's death may be regarded as 'a ransom for many' (Mk. 10:45). . . . When we read of 'redemption through his blood' (Eph. 1:7), the blood of Christ is clearly being regarded as the price of redemption" *(New Bible Dictionary,* p. 1014).

■ Study 2/The Apostle's Prayer

Question 2. The letter now moves from praise to prayer. In Ephesians 1:15 Paul begins an extended prayer which continues right through the next two chapters, ending in 3:21 with the word *Amen.* The prayer form allows the apostle to express deep truths to his readers that perhaps could not be said effectively in any other way. Note, however, that he begins where they are, with words of encouragement and commendation.

Question 6. Although Jesus' position in heaven obviously points to his deity, it also indicates more of his role toward us: "Jesus continues to minister for us. Jesus' resurrection did not separate Him from us. He ascended to be with the Father (Acts 1:9) so that He could send the Holy Spirit to be with each of us (John 16:5-16). He sat down at the Father's right hand as our Priest and Intercessor (Rom. 8:34; Heb. 7:25). In all our troubles believers have an advocate pleading for us with the Father (1 John 2:1). This will be true until He returns to reign eternally" *(Disciple's Study Bible, New International Version,* p. 1667. Nashville: Holman Bible Publishers, 1988).

■ Study 3/Life Out of Death

Question 4. "Important for us is that Satan's power lies behind human rebellion against God. Sinners do not simply rely on human creativity. Satan leads them to devise ways of disobeying God" *(Disciple's Study Bible,* p. 1505).

Question 6. The premise behind this connection between disobedience and wrath is present from the earliest Scriptures. God gave rules and instructions to people that would govern their living together and their relationship to God. People have chosen their own way, and this disobedience against fundamental life principles has resulted in sin-damaged lives. *Wrath* does not necessarily mean that God is waiting to pounce on human error or failure. It is, rather, the natural result of going against the order of God's creation. One preacher explained simply, "God won't bless you when you're going down the wrong road; otherwise you'd stay on that path forever."

Question 10. Ephesians 2:8-10 are among the best-known verses in the Bible that describe *salvation* (along with Romans 10:9-10). Notice that the idea of salvation here involves past, present, and future.

■ Study 4/The End of Old Hostilities

Question 2. When Ephesians was written, there was still the over-riding attitude among Jewish Christians that they (Jews) were really God's people, and non-Jews (Gentiles) had been allowed in. In other words, the Jews had a special "in" where God was concerned. Note Paul's reference to the physical sign of circumcision, which for the Jews was a highly significant mark of national and religious distinction.

Today in the church, there is often a barrier between people who have grown up in a "Christian" environment and those who haven't. Thus the "good" people who have a Christian background tend to have the same attitude the first-century Jewish believers had—that they are God's favorites, and that he allows "other" people into the circle sometimes. This same attitude exists in certain denominations. For the purpose of applying the lesson of this study to our lives, we can substitute for "Gentile" whatever group of people we may assume has no relationship to God.

Question 5. The dividing "wall of hostility" is an allusion to an actual wall that stood in the temple area, symbolizing the eternal separation of Jews from the rest of the human race.

Question 6. Jews claimed the Law (the Ten Commandments and the Levitical law given by Moses) as the distinguishing mark between them and all other people. God had seen fit to give them his own law, and they maintained God's acceptance by obeying it. By abolishing the law as the means of acceptance by God, Jesus has taken away the Jews' reason for pride or exclusivism, and, hence, their "superiority" over others.

Question 10. That the church is founded on the apostles and prophets is important, because it ensures that God's people use as their basis of faith the testimony of those who were special messengers of God or eyewitnesses to the life of Jesus. Anyone can build a church on mere ideas; only as we stay true to the facts of Jesus' birth, life, death, and resurrection can we maintain a church with power that comes from truth in the Holy Spirit.

■ Study 5/A Mystery Revealed

Question 9. "A number of common problems plagued the churches of Asia Minor. . . . First, the heathen religions had to be reckoned with as powerful and growing forces. . . . Second, internal bickering threatened the church itself. The Christians with Jewish backgrounds felt their previous, historical heritage gave them an advantage over Gentiles. This view caused hard feelings within the body of believers. Third, the allure of the world attempted to claim the allegiance of believers because their vocational and financial success often was wrapped up in how they related to the secular world" *(Disciple's Study Bible,* p. 1500). And finally, Paul, their "father" in the faith, was sitting in prison.

■ Study 6/The Gifts of Christ

Question 3. Note that Paul doesn't say there *should be* one body; he says, "There is one body."

Question 8. In the New Testament church, titles are derived from their function. There are no church offices that are merely titles. The purpose of this question is only to yield a cursory discussion of how these particular gifts might manifest themselves. For a deeper personal study of all the spiritual gifts, you may want to refer group members to 1 Corinthians 12, Romans 12, and 1 Peter 4.

■ Study 7/The Old and New Natures

Question 9. Look again at Ephesians 1:13-14, which explains what it means to be *sealed.* First Thessalonians 5:19 says, "Do not put out the Spirit's fire." Grieving the Spirit amounts to working against what the Holy Spirit is trying to do within us and in the world around us.

■ Study 8/Walking in the Light

Question 5. In Matthew 5:14-16, Jesus explains, "You are the light of the world. A city on a hill cannot be hidden. Neither do people light a lamp and put it under a bowl. Instead they put it on its stand, and it gives light to everyone in the house. In the same way, let your light shine before men, that they may see your good deeds and praise your Father in heaven."

■ Study 9/The Marriage Relationship

Question 2. As we see Christ giving himself in service, over and over again, for the sake of the church, it is impossible to see the husband as an authoritarian ruler over the wife. And before the wife is instructed to "submit to" her husband (Ephesians 5:22), both are told to "submit to one another" (verse 21). Although many Bibles break the text between verses 21 and 22, making verse 21 appear to apply only to believers in general, these paragraph breaks were not present in earlier biblical manuscripts.

■ Study 10/Children and Parents, Slaves and Masters

Question 5. Discuss this in as practical a way as possible. It might be helpful in this particular instance to refer to Paul's parallel statement in Colossians 3:21: "Fathers, do not embitter your children, or they will become discouraged."

Question 6. "Slaves played a significant part in this society. There were several million of them in the Roman empire at this time. Because many slaves and owners had become Christians, the early church had to deal straightforwardly with the question of master/slave relations. Paul's statement neither condemns nor condones slavery. Instead, it tells masters and slaves how to live together in Christian households" *(Life Application Bible*, p. 2140. Wheaton, Ill.: Tyndale House Publishers, 1991).

■ Study11/The Christian's Armor

Question 2. "Disciples must struggle with superhuman forms of evil, including Satan. . . . The enemy is an evil spiritual force led by Satan. The enemy includes rulers and authorities, angelic forces created by God through Christ (Col. 1:16) who have rebelled against God and exercise temporary power in our universe. Compare Eph. 1:21; 3:10; Col. 2:15. . . . Evil is not a problem limited to life on earth. Spiritual forces represent Satan's followers who oppose God on His heavenly territory. . . . We can participate in God's victory by identifying with Him and living according to His will (Eph. 5:7-20)" *(Disciple's Study Bible,* p. 1513).

WHAT SHOULD WE STUDY NEXT?

To help your group answer that question, we've listed the Fisherman Guides by category so you can choose your next study.

TOPICAL STUDIES

Angels, Wright

Becoming Women of Purpose, Barton

Building Your House on the Lord, Brestin

Discipleship, Reapsome

Doing Justice, Showing Mercy, Wright

Encouraging Others, Johnson

Examining the Claims of Jesus, Brestin

Friendship, Brestin

The Fruit of the Spirit, Briscoe

Great Doctrines of the Bible, Board

Great Passages of the Bible, Plueddemann

Great Prayers of the Bible, Plueddemann

Growing Through Life's Challenges, Reapsome

Guidance & God's Will, Stark

Heart Renewal, Goring

Higher Ground, Brestin

Lifestyle Priorities, White

Marriage, Stevens

Miracles, Castleman

Moneywise, Larsen

One Body, One Spirit, Larsen

The Parables of Jesus, Hunt

Prayer, Jones

The Prophets, Wright

Proverbs & Parables, Brestin

Satisfying Work, Stevens & Schoberg

Senior Saints, Reapsome

Sermon on the Mount, Hunt

Spiritual Warfare, Moreau

The Ten Commandments, Briscoe

Who Is God? Seemuth

Who Is the Holy Spirit? Knuckles & Van Reken

Who Is Jesus? Van Reken

Witnesses to All the World, Plueddemann

Worship, Sibley

BIBLE BOOK STUDIES

Genesis, Fromer & Keyes

Job, Klug

Psalms, Klug

Proverbs: Wisdom That Works, Wright

Ecclesiastes, Brestin

Jonah, Habakkuk, & Malachi, Fromer & Keyes

Matthew, Sibley

Mark, Christensen

Luke, Keyes

John: Living Word, Kuniholm

Acts 1-12, Christensen

Paul (Acts 13-28), Christensen

Romans: The Christian Story, Reapsome

1 Corinthians, Hummel

Strengthened to Serve (2 Corinthians), Plueddemann

Galatians, Titus & Philemon, Kuniholm

Ephesians, Baylis

Philippians, Klug

Colossians, Shaw

Letters to the Thessalonians, Fromer & Keyes

Letters to Timothy, Fromer & Keyes

Hebrews, Hunt

James, Christensen

1 & 2 Peter, Jude, Brestin

How Should a Christian Live? (1, 2 & 3 John), Brestin

Revelation, Hunt

BIBLE CHARACTER STUDIES

David: Man after God's Own Heart, Castleman

Elijah, Castleman

Great People of the Bible, Plueddemann

King David: Trusting God for a Lifetime, Castleman

Men Like Us, Heidebrecht & Scheuermann

Paul (Acts 13-28), Christensen

Peter, Castleman

Ruth & Daniel, Stokes

Women Like Us, Barton

Women Who Achieved for God, Christensen

Women Who Believed God, Christensen